PASSIVE INCOME TACTICS

Learn Internet Business Insights, Create Multiple Passive Income Streams, and Start Making Money Online (in 3 Months or Less)

POLLUX ANDREWS

Table of Contents

Introduction _____ *4*

Chapter 1: Get Rid of These Passive Income Myths _____ *10*

Chapter 2: You Need to Create A System for Passive Income _____ *19*

Chapter 3: No Money? No Worries- You Can Still Create an Online Business _____ *26*

Chapter 4: The Top Secret to Any Online Business _____ *36*

Chapter 5: What Is Passive Income Content Base? _____ *47*

Chapter 6: How to Effectively Set Up Your Brand's Online Platform _____ *64*

Chapter 7: Write Once, Earn Multiple Times _____ *76*

Chapter 8: Monetize Your Expertise- the Right Way! _____ *84*

Chapter 9: New Default Settings to Scale Up Your Passive Income _____ *90*

Chapter 10: Want to Sell Branded Physical Products? Here You Go! _____ *94*

Conclusion _____ *100*

Introduction

"Passive Income." How many times have you come across this term? I can guarantee that you probably have seen it at least a few times as you look for online income.

The reason is quite obvious. After all, who doesn't want a passive income?

Doesn't it feel great to earn money many times even after putting efforts once? It means you continue to earn money, but you don't have to put efforts multiple times. Robert Kiyosaki smartly quoted once: *"A wealthy person is simply someone who has learned how to make money when they are not working"*

Precisely, passive income ensures that you don't trade your time for money. Therefore, you can spend the time earned through your passive income pursuits in exploring more opportunities about business, adventures or life in general. You can enjoy time with your family, friends and loved ones, without worrying about being physically present to earn money.

All this Sounds pretty cool, isn't it?

Therefore, everyone wants passive income and the lifestyle it can give to you. And precisely due to this reason, there is so much material out there about how to earn passive income or earn money online or work from home etc. etc.

Passive Income: Hype or Real System?

If you're reading this book, chances are, you probably have been exposed to lots of YouTube videos and books targeting this phrase. But, if you have bothered to investigate such resources, you probably have found out first hand that many such materials are not that good.

In fact, many of them are hyped, exaggerated and heavily promoted. There's a lot of smoke and heat. But unfortunately, if you are the typical online passive income seeker, you probably did not get much light.

You are hardly alone. **The fact is, there's a lot of hype out there**. People talk a good game. There are all sorts of products and courses claiming to teach you the ins and outs of building an online passive income.

Don't get fooled. While many of them no doubt contain actual useful information, if you take action on them, you might still end up failing.

I know this is hard to believe. After all, if you do a good job weeding out the fakes, the scams, the hype, you probably would be left with the stuff that works. But I'm sad to say, that even if you follow the stuff that actually works, you might still end up with very little to show for your efforts.

How come? Well, **these products teach you how to do individual things**. These things might even lead to money from time to time. That's not the problem. The hard truth is, you cannot rely on hacks. And that is precisely what you get with a typical passive income online resource. **You get hacks.**

What are "hacks?" They are **cheap, quick, and all too temporary ways** to stack some cash off the internet.

You're not looking to make money here and there. Because if that's all you're in it for, you're probably already doing that right now. You can try freelancing. There are all sorts of stuff you can do online that delivers cash from time to time.

But that's not what you're looking for. You're looking for something more **permanent.** You're looking for something more **stable**. You're looking for **actual income**.

Sadly, the vast majority of affiliate marketing guides out there, as well as passive income courses and seminars, fail to deliver. They deliver hacks.

But if you are really serious, you should be doing something else. You should be building a business system. Let me repeat that again. You have to **build a business system**. Otherwise, you're just wasting your time online.

This Book is About Real Passive Income Business System

This book teaches you how to create a real passive income business in a systematic and methodical way. We will start you with building a "base business" from your existing interests. Once you get that going, you will then scale up to create an interlocking, self-sustaining passive income ecosystem.

In other words, when you create content, it draws traffic which leads to your other properties, which then draws traffic that leads to your other properties, and so on and so forth.

This way, when you create an ecosystem, you end up recycling traffic. You end up building a sustainable brand, and avoid wasting time and effort. Compare this with a typical online income guide that teaches you hack after hack after hack.

Believe me, I've bought products that supposedly teach people how to make money instantly. Some of those products actually worked. But pay attention to the word I used, it's in past tense. It wasn't scalable. And sooner or later, the hack no longer worked.

You can't live your life that way. You can't build a real business on a foundation of hacks. You have to build a system.

This book is very different from other books and resources that focus on passive income on the internet. **This is not about hacks**. This is not some sort of one-trick pony that you just have to ride to success. This is not some sort of cash cow that you build and continue to milk until it goes dry.

Instead, you learn how to build an actual business. You can choose to scale it up or you can replicate the system that I will teach you and apply it to many different niches. It's all up to you.

The good news is, when you're building your business this way, you end up with an asset. People buy assets. They don't buy hacks because they know that these are shallow and don't last all that long. Know the difference.

This book teaches you **how to build an asset that you can later on sell for a huge amount of money**. That's where it leads to. Instead of just a temporary "hack" that makes money from time to time, you end up building a self-reinforcing and self-sustaining system that generates revenue over the long haul.

Of course, it takes quite a bit of a commitment. It takes time, and yes, it takes effort. It may take very little money to set up, but you have to focus on solving problems, doing the right research, and putting in the work.

In other words, this is a **real business**. It's not some sort of "done for you" scam product. This is not an "autopilot" business that you can just set up and leave alone. You have to learn the ropes. And once you know how everything works out, you can then keep replicating the system.

The good news is, once you master how everything works, it becomes easier and easier to scale up the system or create businesses in other niches. I'll see you in Chapter 1.

Chapter 1: Get Rid of These Passive Income Myths

Make no mistake, there are lots of myths about making money online that not only wastes your time, but ensures your poverty. I know that sounds crazy, but you have to understand that what you believe will help you or prevent you in your efforts to achieve.

That's right, it doesn't matter whether you are trying to get better grades in school, create better relationships or become more physically fit, if you let the wrong ideas into your head, your results are going to suffer. It's only a matter of time.

The same applies to your efforts at trying to make money online passively. Believe the following lies, myths and legends and you'll go broke trying to get rich or stay broke. Neither of these situations is good, so listen up.

Myth #1: Passive income systems can make you rich quickly

The Reality: Passive income systems are businesses

I'm sure you're probably not under the delusion that the moment you build some sort of website that the money will start rushing in. Most sensible people don't operate this way. Most people are quite realistic in their expectations.

The problem is, there seems to be a genre or a niche online called "make money online" or MMO that seems so aggressive in the hype department that it's creating more problems than it solves. It really is.

Why? Well, if you take a lot of these sales pages at face value, you can't help but walk away with a conclusion that you just need to put up some sort of website or system by following their instructions and you will get rich. After all, that is what the sales copy says.

But the problem is, these aggressive sales copies are intended to make you do one thing and one thing alone: to buy their product.

The reality is actually quite a letdown. The reality is anticlimactic. What is the reality? Well, online marketing is a business.

That's right. You're forced to solve people's problems, you're supposed to pay attention to what you're doing, you're supposed to make certain changes, and you have to commit to the long haul.

Where's the fun in that? Where's the automated income in that? Where are the instant riches? There is none. It's work. After all, it's a business.

And this is why, if you think that putting up a passive income system will somehow make all your financial problems go away, you are just making things harder for yourself. You really are. You are setting yourself up for a big disappointment.

Passive income systems are still businesses. Treat them as such. They take time to build, optimize and grow. Prepare yourself accordingly.

Myth #2: Passive income systems are fully passive

The Reality: You need to invest work and time to build and operate passive income systems

There are lots of books out there, in particular, Tim Ferris' 4-Hour Work Week. Can you imagine getting 40 hours worth of results with only 4 hours worth of work? Sounds awesome, right? Who wouldn't be excited? Who wouldn't get all pumped up about freeing up 36 hours so they can spend it on their loved ones or living a more fulfilling life?

But unfortunately, there's a lot in the fine print. While it's true that Tim Ferris might have been able to create such a lifestyle for himself, most people don't start out that way. What the title of Feriss' book doesn't tell you is that it took a lot of work and focus and attention to detail to get to that point. He didn't start there.

Keep this in mind because it's easy to think that since passive income building is all about working once to create an asset and reaping the results many times over, there is absolutely no follow up work needed. Alternatively, the thinking is that you don't really have to put in that much work.

As I've mentioned in Myth #1, this is still a business. Businesses require work. If you're a business person, your number one job is to solve problems.

Let me clue you in on a harsh reality: you need to invest work and time to build an online passive income system. You then have to invest time to optimize. Once your system is working and has scaled up to a certain level, then you can work less and less. Regardless of how far along it is in terms of its development and evolution, you still have to invest time and effort.

Here's the clincher: there's no such thing as a fully passive online income system, except for domain speculation or intellectual property rights investments. Outside of that, you have to still put in some work. At the very least, if your system is highly advanced and pretty much fully developed, you would still have to invest a few hours every week or every month to keep the money flowing in.

Myth #3: Passive income systems require absolutely zero cash

The Reality: You need domains and hosting for most online income systems

While it is possible that you can start out your passive income empire using free resources like social media platforms and free blogging platforms like WordPress or blogger.com, eventually, you would have to buy a domain. Eventually, you would have to have a home for your brand.

Don't get me wrong, I'm not saying that you cannot make money with absolutely no cash on the internet. I've done it before. People I've known have done it. But we were using primarily hacks.

The way we were making money was fairly shallow and superficial. In other words, we weren't building brands. We were not building a solid online presence. We didn't bother to do any of that.

Instead, we were using quick hit-and-run short-cuts using free resources to make a few bucks here and there. It's really hard to scale up using this approach.

The good news is, it doesn't take much money to build a fairly serious online passive income empire. Seriously.

Compared to the typical brick and mortar business models like restaurants, online income systems are dirt cheap. You basically just need to invest in hosting and domains.

Hosting, in particular, is very, very scalable. You can cram 50 different sites in one fairly cheap hosting package and not suffer any kind of deterioration in performance.

Make no mistake, if you are looking to make money online, passive income systems is a great place to start. They require fairly low levels of investment. Your main investment is your time.

Myth #4: Passive income systems are "set it and forget it" systems

The Reality: You need to pay attention to the business you have built

There is a subset of online course builders and promoters who have come up with all sorts of products to take advantage of people. They're focused on people who are not willing to learn. They're focused on people who are simply looking to buy businesses instead of starting them, researching them, and growing them from scratch. This is where the whole "set it and forget it" sub niche of the whole make money online niche arose.

But the problem here is that if you are looking to enjoy real passive income systems, you have to treat them the way they should be treated. You have to treat them like businesses.

In other words, you need to pay attention to them. You need to optimize them for optimal revenue and traffic generation. You also have to scale them up. That's why I can tell you with no hesitation, that there is no such thing as a "set it and forget it" system.

You have to set it up, pay attention to what works, build on it, and disregard what doesn't work. You then optimize your system so that it generates as much cash as possible, then you scale it up both within your niche and outside your niche. That's how it works. In other words, it's a business.

The great thing about it is that you can manage it on your own terms. You can get around to it when you have the time. It gives you a tremendous amount of flexibility. You can travel all over the world and not have to worry about showing up to an office and punching the clock and suffering through 8 hours of office work.

Still, regardless of the freedom of mobility and time management, you still have to put in the time. You still have to put in the work. There's no such thing as a "set it and forget it" income system. If you've seen those sales pages, disregard them. Seriously.

I'm not saying that they're all scams. I'm sure some of them work. But the problem is, they are based on one person or a couple of person's experience. And the sales page makes that experience, which is fairly rare and usually requires a tremendous amount of skill and talent, appear to apply to everybody else. It doesn't work that way.

So forget about maximizing convenience and saving a huge amount of time. Focus instead of finding a model that works for you.

Myth #5: Passive income systems can be "done for you"

The Reality: Others can set up your business, but you still need to run it

Don't get me wrong, I have nothing against "done for you" systems. These are online businesses that are put up by professional business builders. That's what they do. That's what they're all about.

They find online business opportunities, create a business around those opportunities, and then hand off the business to a buyer. Nothing wrong with that. In fact, brick and mortar businesses operate the same way. The problem lies with the buyer.

If you approach this whole situation with the expectation that since you bought your business and you just basically have to babysit it while it throws up cash, then you are setting yourself up for a disappointment. Seriously. You're just setting yourself up for a letdown sooner rather than later.

Why? Well, you bought a business. You have to handle it accordingly.

Problems will appear. You cannot let them fester. You cannot let them grow. You cannot let them get cancerous.

Also, opportunities present themselves all the time. You need to take advantage of these. Also, when you are running your system, make sure you look at building on your strengths and working on areas for improvement.

In other words, just because somebody has handed you a business that actually works, it doesn't automatically mean that you should just coast and let things run. It can still fail. You have to handle it the way it needs to be handled. It's still a business.

Chapter 2: You Need to Create A System for Passive Income

Considering the huge amount of online income products out there that teach you how to turn online traffic into cold, hard dollars, why even mess around with systems? What is it about building a system that is worthy of your time, attention and effort? Why should you build a system when you can just rely on money making hacks, shortcuts or "automated cash machine" gimmicks?

Well, while these alternatives, at some level or another do work (some better than others), systems blow them all away. Let me repeat that. There are lots of alternative models for making money online currently available on the market, but if you build a system, you will still have a business at the end of the day.

I can't say the same for the alternatives. Why? Well, pay attention to the following reasons.

Systems are Intentional

Let's get one thing clear, given how awesome the internet is, it's not unusual for complete and total idiots or clueless people to make a lot of money. Seriously. People can and do hit the lotto.

The same goes with making online riches. I know people who are not all that intelligent nor intellectually curious, but they made their fair share of money along the way.

Unfortunately, if we were to rewind the tape, so to speak, a lot of these people would not know the first thing about making money online. They got lucky.

Just as a lottery winner may have picked other numbers, if you rewound the tape, people who made six to seven or even eight figures off the internet are not exactly guaranteed that they would enjoy the same fortune if their situations were even slightly different.

To avoid this randomness, you should build a system. Passive income systems are intentional in nature. You basically understand why things work. You are looking for specific outcomes and building processes that generate that outcome.

You also create passive income systems that build on each other. In other words, one part creates content and some traffic. This then is fed to another part that creates more traffic than content, and they end up complementing each other.

This is how system builders work. They don't just look at one hack after another. They don't just look at quick and shallow victories.

Let me tell you, there are lots of people out there who made a lot of money on the internet and just as quickly lost that money. The worst part? They're flat on their backs now. They don't know how to make the "magic" happen again. The reason? They didn't build a system.

Systems Lead to More Income

Since systems are focused on building an interlocking network of content and traffic generation processes, it is no surprise that passive income systems lead to more money. They're interlocking. Whatever brand you build with one end, you get traffic with the other end. You also recycle your traffic.

For example, if you first start with YouTube videos, you can then transcribe those videos into blog posts. You can then turn those posts into tweets. You can also turn those posts into Facebook page updates. You can turn those posts into Facebook group updates.

You can also turn this content into pictures that you post on Instagram or Pinterest. You can create infographics from the diagrams you come up with in your blog posts and publish this on Pinterest and your Facebook page. This is how you create an interlocking ecosystem that feeds content and traffic all over the place.

All these activities end up reinforcing your brand. Instead of just doing one thing and hoping for the best, you do one thing and it starts a chain reaction throughout the ecosystem that you've built for yourself.

Now, you probably won't get far with just one post, but can you imagine if you were consistently building content?

That's how solid brands are built. They use a system. They just don't rely on being lucky.

You can try being lucky by trying to come up with a viral video, but let me tell you, that's like trying to freeze lightning. I'm sure it happens from time to time, but given how random and improbable that is, it's probably not worth doing.

Systems are Self-Sustaining

As I've mentioned above, if you build a massive base of content and you promote it halfway decently, you start creating a traffic flow from many different places. I am of course talking about social media, forums, question and answer sites, and other online resources that can send traffic your way.

You don't have to pay for this organic traffic. Eventually, if you get enough content and you format your content right and get some backlinks along the way, you also stand to gain a nice flow of passive search engine traffic.

Now, if you build a system, you're not just going to sit back and wait for all this traffic to hit your website and flow through. Instead, since you're thinking systematically, you're going to direct some of that traffic deeper and deeper into your blog, and then direct them to your YouTube channel, your Facebook page, your Facebook groups, your Twitter account, and so on and so forth.

In other words, you create an internal chain reaction of traffic that ends up reinforcing your brand while increasing your chances of getting ad clicks at the same time.

Systems are Self Reinforcing

If you know what you're doing, when people come into contact with your content on social media, they can click and end up getting branded again and again.

When they click, they can go to your blog. On your blog, you can direct them to your YouTube channel. On your YouTube channel, you can direct them to your other branded presence on the internet.

In other words, you keep sending them the message that you're not some sort of fly by night, shady operator. You keep sending them the message that not only do you know what you're talking about, but you can be trusted.

Now, let me tell you, which operator would consumers trust more? Somebody that happens to give them the information that they are looking for every once in a while, or somebody that they can keep coming back to as a resource regarding a specific category of information? It's not even close.

People prefer brands. At the back of their heads, they start thinking that they have a relationship with your brand. They feel that they can trust you with certain types of information.

This is the kind of brand relationship you're looking for because it increases trust. You can then convert that trust, sooner or later, into actual dollars.

Systems can be Self-Optimizing

The great thing about building a system is that you not only start a chain reaction that leads to more conversions down the road, but you also set up a system where you can collect valuable consumer intelligence. Because whatever lessons you learn in one part of your online passive income empire, maybe it's your blog, you can then apply it to other parts of your system.

For example, on your blog, people can leave comments. Pay attention to your community's comments. Apply some of these lessons on your social media accounts and see if your social media content would enjoy greater engagement. Once you see all of this in action, you can then keep fine tuning your online passive income empire, thanks to this free feedback.

This is how systems optimize themselves. But they have to be set up properly.

In Chapter 3, I'm going to step you through the process of starting up your online passive income empire assuming that you have absolutely no cash to start with.

Chapter 3: No Money? No Worries- You Can Still Create an Online Business

Generally speaking, when people start a business they either have seed capital ready, or they know where to find it. Maybe they have friends and family, they can talk to. Maybe they can get a loan.

Whatever the case may be; usually, when people look to build a business they know that money is needed, and they usually have an idea where the money is going to come from.

Now, if you are thinking of putting up an online income system that generates money passively, but you have absolutely no money — it's not the end. It's okay. If you have absolutely no cash right now, you can still build your passive online income empire.

This is what separates this type of business from the typical brick and mortar business. Believe me. If you are thinking of putting up a bakery, a restaurant, a barber shop, or something else, you better know where to get your capital.

Otherwise, it's not going to happen. Not so with passive online income systems. Here's how you do it.

Identify Skills You May Have That People Will Pay For

Do you know how to do something that people will pay money for? It doesn't have to be a lot of money; mind you, as long as they're willing to pay you to do something. Maybe you are good at graphics, you can create banners, ebook covers, or website headers.

Maybe you know how to write, even if you have fairly weak writing skills. Maybe you know enough to rewrite somebody else's work. Maybe you have a nice voice; if so, you can record voice-overs.

These are recordings of you reading a prepared script. Maybe you are easy on the eyes; if so, you can be an online spokesperson. That's right. You can read from a teleprompter, or read from notes in front of you, and record a speech on camera.

There're so many ways you can turn your skill set and time into dollars. Thanks to places like fiverr.com, upwork.com, and freelancer.com. You have a wide range of options, when it comes to selling your time. That's really what freelancing boils down to.

You're going to be selling your time. Also, if you have skills that require interaction with the real world: like handing out fliers, taking pictures, interviewing people. You can also do this. You can also offer these services on freelance platforms.

The secret is reinvesting

The next step is to reinvest your money. This is the key. If you have absolutely no cash to start your online passive income system, that's perfectly okay. You just have to reinvest some portion of your earnings back into your passive income system. You have to remember this part.

The Harsh Truth About Freelancing

The harsh reality of freelancing is that it's very easy to get addicted to it. Believe me. I ought to know. When I first started earning money off the Internet, I was writing for a lot of people. I love to write. I love to research, and I basically look at my freelance job as getting paid to learn.

Since I'm a very curious person, this was the very best job in the world for me. Now, here's the problem, I get so focused on freelancing that I get stuck. I quickly cross the line between freelancing only to the extent that I generate cash to fund my online income systems to treating it as a job.

Let me tell you, if you are freelancing, and you're treating it as a job — you are in a tough spot. Seriously. The great thing about the typical job in the United States is that you don't just get paid a certain hourly wage. That's actually the tip of the iceberg.

You also get a wide range of benefits. You can get health coverage, dental insurance, life insurance. You name it. And this is precisely what you're missing when you're freelancing, and unfortunately if you completely lose focus and view your freelancing as activities as your main job, you're actually losing out.

You're better off getting an actual job. No joke. This is why it's really important to have a freelance escape plan, or a freelance system. This system is intended to help you set aside enough of your hours, so you can direct those hours to building your online passive income empire. Here is my suggestion.

Breaking free from freelancing

Assuming that you're reinvesting some of your freelance income into building your passive income system, then the next step is to determine the least amount of hours you can freelance, so you can focus on building your business. The key here is to determine the number of hours you need to freelance to take care of your bills.

I'm not just talking about the rent, the mortgage, the kids' private school, tuition, your gas, your car note — if you have one, any insurance bills and whatnot. I'm also not talking exclusively about food and other recurring expenses. I want you to come up with your total bill for the month and add 10%, or 20%. That's going to be your "cushion."

Once, you have that total number, break that down into the number of freelancing hours you have to absolutely put in, so you can take care of your household. Once you're crystal clear on that number, commit the rest of your time to building a passive income system. This is how you break free from freelancing.

Since, you know that if you work load in a certain number of hours every month, you are taking precious time away from your passive income empire. This acts as some sort of dividing line.

The key here is to put as much time into passive income building, so you will produce enough assets, that sooner or later these assets will actually produce most of your income. Also, the more time you put into this type of activity, the sooner you will break free from freelancing.

I know people who started freelancing, and after about six months, they were able to completely live off their passive income assets. I'm not talking about barely getting by. I'm not talking about making costly sacrifices. I'm talking about just pure income replacement. These people are making six figures every single year. It can be done.

But, you have to have a system for breaking free from freelancing. You can start with zero. That's fine. But you must not stay with freelancing. Otherwise, you're just making things harder on yourself. You're actually putting yourself at a serious disadvantage if you rely primarily on freelancing for your main income.

The Secret to a Quick Transition From Freelancing To Passive Income

I know, I told you that, I know several people personally who started out as freelancers, and are now enjoying fully passive income. They're doing quite well. But, I wish I could tell you, that this is the case across the board.

Unfortunately, this is far from true; for every one person that is able to transition from freelancing to purely passive income are a lot more people who are stuck in the freelance game, or who have simply quit and gone back to their nine-to-five jobs.

What is the secret to a quick and effective transition from freelancing to passive income? There are three factors that are in play: first, you have to have the discipline. The great thing about freelancing is also the worst thing about it. When you're freelancing, you don't have a boss.

You don't have a supervisor that's looking over your shoulder and telling you what to do. Now, this is great if you're a self-starter, but this can be catastrophic if you are the type of person who needs structure and constant guidance. If you're the latter type, you need to build discipline.

You have to set things up that you don't need much guidance, or threatening emails from your clients to deliver stuff on time. I know this is quite a tall order, especially if you don't have that type of personality. But, the good news is the sooner you start on this, the better off you would be.

The next thing that you need to work on is your focus. As the old saying goes; where your focus goes — energy flows. When you focus on building a business, you know that that is your end goal.

You know that this is your destiny. Compare this with focusing on making enough dollars on a month-to-month basis, so you can pay the rent or your mortgage. If that is your focus, then what do you think happens to your dreams of financial independence. That's right. It goes up in smoke. It really does.

Again, where your focus goes — energy flows. All your energy is focused on getting by. I'm telling you, if that's the case, get a job, seriously. In the United States, there are more jobs than there are people, so you have no excuse.

But, if you are serious about building an online passive income empire, focus on that. Don't focus on your freelancing. Again, I'm not saying that you should completely drop the ball and be totally irresponsible. I'm not saying that.

What I am saying is that, you should stick to the minimum number of hours you would need to put in, so you can take care of your bills. You still have to be a responsible adult, but the rest of your time should be focused like a laser on what matters most: Building a business.

Finally, you have to become more efficient. I remember when I first started freelancing, I would take all day, seriously. I thought, I was on vacation, so I would basically just go around. Also, since I picked my projects, I developed a really big ego. If the prospective client rubbed me the wrong way, I would not take their project.

It doesn't matter whether they're paying thousands of dollars to get something done. I would let my emotions get the better of me. Well, after having done that for quite some time, a few things dawned on me.

First of all, freelancing is a feast or famine proposition. Don't believe for a second that just because you're popular among your clients that the gravy train will continue to roll forever. It doesn't work that way.

Sometimes you just hit a hot streak. I remember when I made $50,000 in the span of three months, it blew my mind. I mean it still shocks me from time to time, but guess what happened after that point, I did not get a winning bid on a project for several months.

Again, feast or famine. This is why it's really important to become really efficient when you're freelancing. You don't really know when the big contracts will come, or if you already have a big contract when these contracts would end.

So, in the meantime, your focus should be on maximizing the amount of results you get for whatever time you invest in your freelance practice. This means, investing in automation like software. This also means hiring assistants.

Remember, if you are freelancing you are trading your time for money. The best way to do this is to charge a higher amount of money per unit of time, and then subcontract some of the work. Of course, you still have to sign on the dotted line, and you are still ultimately responsible for the quality of your output. That's not going to go away any time soon.

However, by hiring assistants whether on site or virtual assistants you leverage other people's time. This way, instead of having only 40 hours to sell week after week you can theoretically sell 200, 400, or even more hours. See how this works.

Of course, when you hire assistants you also have to develop project management skills. It's not like you can treat these people the way you treat your projects. You can't develop "spoiled artists mindset" and expect all of this to fly.

Finally, establish a solid reputation for quality. If you really want to quickly transition from freelancing to passive income, you have to build a brand for your services. If you're able to do this, people are willing to pay a premium for every unit of time you spend doing their job. That's how it works.

And, if you're able to do this since people are paying a nice premium per hour unit of work done, you can then turn around, and hire other people to do parts of the work. This is how you explode your profit margin. With enough money and enough deficiency, you can then spend an increasing amount of your time to doing what you should have been doing all along: Building passive income systems.

Chapter 4: The Top Secret to Any Online Business

I know, if you're reading this book, you probably have read all sorts of online income guides. You had probably even signed up for an online income seminar or two. Believe me, I talked to my customers, and they tell me the same story.

The problem is, when it comes time for them to actually build their online passive income business, they end up failing. How come? They neglected one important stuff. It's not like they're completely blind to it. It's not like they're completely unaware of it or nobody told them.

The problem is, it was put in front of their face, and they treated it as some sort of formality. That's right. They just blew through it. At the back of their heads, they're thinking, I already know what I want, I know what works, I know that this is going to make me millions of dollars.

Well, I'm telling you if that's your mindset, you better check yourself before you wreck yourself. No joke. Your assumptions can lead the way to you blowing through the most important step of building any kind of online income. This is a mistake you cannot afford to make. What am I talking about, I'm talking about: Niche selection.

You can screw up all the other parts of the online income business building system, but if you screw this part up, you're toast. Seriously. Kiss your dreams of making dollars off the internet, goodbye. It's that simple. It's that final. It's that devastating.
What's so important about niche selection anyways?

Well, if you are wondering why online passive incomes depend on niche selection so much, you have to understand what niches' relationship to your income generating capabilities are. First of all, your niche determines your income. That's right. Different niches have different products, and people have different levels of willingness to pay good money for those products.

For certain niche products people are not willing to pay much money at all. For others, they're willing to pay a huge amount of cash. You have to know the difference. You have to focus on selecting a niche that has enough commercial value so as to make it worth your time. In other words, to borrow a phrase from a famous bank robber, "Go where the money is."

Next, niches determined the size of your audience. Some niches attract a lot of people. Their markets are very big and the audience size plays a big role and how much money you will make. They kind of go hand in hand. If you have an audience of a million people, and they're willing to pay you a dollar per month, that's a million dollars in potential income every month.

Now, if people are only willing to pay $1, but that audience size has been reduced to let's say 1,000 people; you will only be making as much as $1,000 from your audience. Which audience would you rather have? The choice is rather obvious.

Finally, niche selection determines how scalable your niche is. There are certain niches where people expect to buy many products in sequence. Take the case of 10,000 people in a niche where products cost $1. You may be thinking that this is a non-starter, because the total commercial value of that niche on a monthly basis is $10,000.

Well, look more closely. If it turns out that people in that niche have made it a habit to buy product after product, you're not just looking at $10,000 per month. You might possibly be looking at six figures, or even seven figures month after month. Scalability is crucial.

HOW DO YOU SELECT A NICHE?

Now that you have a clear idea of how important niche selection is to building your online passive income system, how exactly do you pick out a niche? In the following series of steps, I'm going to walk you through the process of picking a niche that makes a lot of sense for you personally. This is not some sort of one-size-fits-all cookie cutter solution.

There is no magic bullet solution here that applies to all people at all times to produce the same results. This is not hype after all. This is reality. Follow the steps that I shared with you below, and you will be sure to pick out a niche that makes all the sense in the world for you.

Step #1:
List your personal passions

It doesn't matter whether you're freelancing, finding work or building a passive income system, it has to make sense to you personally. I'm a firm believer in the idea that if a person loves what they do, they will produce better work. This means, with everything else being equal, they're more likely to be successful.

It's only a matter of time until you start hating what you do if you were never passionate about it to begin with. This leads to you producing lower quality work or viewing work like some sort of chore. I'm telling you that is not the way to build an online passive income empire. Your empire would be built on a foundation of dust. It's only a matter of time until it crashes like a house of cards.

Do it right the first time around by building your system on your personal passions. How do you do this? Well, think about all the things you love to talk about and then write them down. Off the top of your head, just write down the topics you would talk about even if you were not getting paid. That's how passionate you are about these topics.

There are no right or wrong answers here, so don't edit yourself. Just write down the first thing that comes to mind, fill up that piece of paper, flip it around, fill up the back, get another piece and keep doing this until you run out of ideas. Remember, your only filter is that you like talking about this stuff. You are interested in this stuff.

Step #2

Filter by commercial value

Now that you have a list of topics that you like to talk about, the next step is to log on to Google AdWords and use their Google Keyword Planner Tool. With this tool, type in the keywords related to the topics you love talking about. When you do this, you would notice that, for some of the keywords, dollar values would appear. The Google Keyword Planner Tool is giving you a rough guess on the commercial value of these keywords. Pay attention to these. List these next to your list of keywords on your sheet.

Now, at this point, eliminate niches or topics that have very low commercial value on average. I'm talking about averages here. Sure, maybe one keyword for that niche would fetch $10 a click. But if everything is else is south of 10¢, you're in trouble. Those topics may not have enough commercial value to deliver a positive return on effort, as well as ROI.

Step #3

Filter by demand volume

At this point, your list should be getting shorter. That's a good sign. Now it's going to get even shorter. Using the Google Keyword Planner Tool, enter the remaining keywords and pay attention to their search volume every single month. Eliminate niches that have fairly low commercial value in relation to their search volume.

If you notice that a particular topic has a lower than the average search volume but have very high commercial value, hang on to those. Also, you should obviously hang on to keywords that have high volumes and a high commercial value. For everything else, scratch them off your list.

Step #4

Filter by competition

Using Google Search, enter all the keywords that are remaining on your list. Eliminate topics that have too many websites targeting them. When you search for a keyword on Google, it will tell you the number of results you got. These are roughly the number of websites competing for that keyword. If the number is too high, eliminate that topic from your list.

Once you're done with this, go to YouTube and do the same. If you notice that there are too many videos competing for the same keyword, eliminate that topic from your list.

Step #5

Filter by trend

Get on Google Trends and plug in the remaining keywords you have on your list. Look at the trend line. Do you see it going up over time or do you see it sinking over time? If the trend line is flat or ramping up over time, hang on to that topic. Get rid of everything else. You want to target niches that will continue to be around long into the future.

You don't want to target a niche that is somehow dying. If you need proof of this, try to look up fidget spinners. Remember those? Those were all the rage a couple of years back. Nowadays, nobody would want to be caught dead with them. That's how unpopular they have become. They have fallen out of fashion. Can you imagine building an online store empire on fidget spinners? Talk about a waste of time. Focus on niches that are scaling up.

SECOND LEVEL COMPETITION RESEARCH

After you have done the main filtering above, the next step is to investigate the competition among your remaining niches more finely. At this point, it's too easy to think that you have great niches to work with. It's very tempting to think that you just need to focus on these and you are in the free and clear. This is absolutely wrong.

You also have to look at secondary competition signals. Again, you use these to filter whatever is left.

Ideally, you should have started with a massive list of topics. By this point, you should still have a dozen or two left. The good news is that you will be able to zero in like a laser on the niches that are worth pursuing after you do the secondary competition level research. Here are the steps.

Step #1

Find the number of existing YouTube videos for your niches

Just get a number of existing videos and write that number down next to each niche keyword.

Step #2

Find the number of existing social media accounts

Enter your topic keywords into Facebook, Twitter or Pinterest and collect the total number of social media accounts that target your specific keywords. Put these numbers next to you list of niches.

Step #3

Find the number of existing Kindle books

Enter your keywords one by one into Amazon Kindle Book Store. You should be able to retrieve all sorts of Kindle books. Just pay attention to the number of titles appearing and list these. Also pay attention to the sales ranks of those books. The lower the numerical score, the better. The closer a book is to #1, the higher its rank.

For Kindle competition analysis, you should have two numbers. The first number is the number of books competing in that niche. The second number is the average sales rank of those books.

Step #4

Find the number of Udemy channels

Go to Udemy, create an account and search through their system regarding the number of courses that people are offering targeting your niches. Record the number for each of these.

FINDING YOUR SWEET SPOT

Now that you have done your research, here comes the hard part. You're going to have to select one of your research niches to begin with. The key here is to select a niche that you're passionate about, has decent demand, and had great commercial value. The niche must also have manageable levels of competition.

If you did your homework correctly, you should be able to zero in on one niche that stands out. If you're stuck in a situation where you have a handful of niches that basically have the same scores, use your heart.

When you look at the topics, which ones are the most personally interesting to you? Pick that one.

Chapter 5: What Is Passive Income Content Base?

At this point, a lot of the typical affiliate marketing and passive income building guides out there would get you all excited about blogging. In their minds, this the logical place to start. You basically do some keyword research, find content in your niche and then create content. It's pretty straightforward. That's the conventional wisdom.

Well, that couldn't be further from the truth. Get that out of your head. If you're going to build a system, do it the way I'm going to teach you.

Create Passive Video Content To Create A Base Income

The first thing that you need to do is to create videos. I know that cuts against the grain, but let me tell you, the great thing about creating videos is that you are building assets that grow in value over time. Sure, you're not making money off them on day 1. YouTube had changed its rules regarding monetizing content.

YouTube will only pay you per 1000 views if your channel has gotten more than 4000 hours of use and has at least a certain number of subscribers. These are the two key qualification points you need for YouTube, otherwise you're not going to make passive money from it. This is why a lot of people avoid YouTube, but I suggest you start with it.

The reason for this is that the more video content you upload and the more you promote them, the sooner you get past that initial monetization threshold. Once you're able to do that, you can then repurpose your YouTube video content to build the rest of your passive income empire. This way you save a tremendous amount of time.

A lot of people have it exactly in reverse. They build their social media presence first and then they get around to video, assuming they get around to it. This really is too bad because it leaves a lot of money on the table. Believe me, 4000 hours of video views take a while to build up. That's why you need to get on it sooner rather than later. Build your system on video first and then everything else will fall into place. Here is how you do it.

How YouTube Video Content Passive Income Works?

Before I step you through the process of building videos that make you money on YouTube, how exactly does the system work? Well, if you spend any time on YouTube, you know that they make their money off advertising. When you watch a video, after some time, an ad will appear. Then, if you keep watching, another ad will appear. Also, when you are scrolling through the video collections, there are certain places for ads.

This is how Google makes money off YouTube. Well, YouTube will pay you for a percentage of the views your channel gets. The more videos you upload to your channel and the more people view your videos, all this adds up to viewing time. Generally speaking, this payment can range anywhere from $1 per thousand views to $10 or more. It all depends on where your visitors are coming from and the niche of your videos among other factors.

This is why it's really important to build a channel and load it with as many videos as possible and then promote those videos. It may well turn out that each of these videos don't really get that many views. But since you have so many videos uploaded over an extended period of time and more and more people discover them, all these views can add up.

Sure, it may seem like you're making only $2.50 per thousand views. But if you have so many videos and so many people have heard of your videos so that it starts to scale up, your $2.50 might easily turn into $2500 per month or more. The best part to all of this is you don't have to lift a finger to make more money off the videos you have already uploaded.

You just need to create them, upload them, promote them, move on to the next video and then the next video after that. The extra bonus here is if you have developed a solid brand for your videos, it becomes easier and easier for people to look for your newer videos. If you play your cards right, this can drive up the earning power of your older video collection.

How to make money using YouTube videos

Unfortunately, to get an AdSense account, you have to get 4000 hours of views on your video. You also have to get a certain number of channel subscribers. Once these are out of the way, you can then sign up for YouTube's monetization program. Now, please note that YouTube will review your application. It doesn't guarantee that you will get accepted.

The only thing that they can guarantee is that they would review your application. This is why it's really important to be as professional as possible. Follow the steps below to increase your chances of getting accepted into YouTube's revenue sharing system because you are a legit operation. Make no mistake, there are a lot of scammers and impersonators on YouTube. That's why they have these rules in the first place. But if you follow everything I tell you below, you should be good to go.

Create a professional-looking channel

The first thing that you need to do after you have selected your target niche is to create a professional-looking channel for your brand on YouTube. Thankfully, this is actually cheaper than you think. You just need to head on over to Fiverr. There are lots of professional cover makers and designers out there who would build you a nice-looking channel cover for all of $5.

It's also important that you describe your channel well. This is crucial. You can't just blow through this. You can't just go through the motions. You have to clearly explain to people what they should expect from your channel. What exactly would your videos be about? What kind of experience do you deliver? What kind of value should they expect?

You have to answer these questions because it doesn't really matter what niche you're in, chances are, you're not going to be the only person targeting that niche. You have to come up with a unique selling proposition, which convinces your prospective viewers to stick to your channel and possibly become a subscriber.

Create videos that add value to your viewers' lives

It's really important to make sure that you create videos that people would want to watch. I can't even begin to tell you how many YouTube "moneymaking guides" I've read throughout the years. A lot of them are basically garbage. That's all they are. They tell you that you should just come up with garbage videos and target all sorts of keywords and fill up YouTube with that trash.

They're saying that even if one video gets just one view a day, since you have thousands upon thousands of videos, eventually, this translates to a big paycheck. It makes me horribly sad to even think of the people who have actually taken that advice. Talk about a massive waste of time. You have to understand that YouTube is not run by idiots.

If they notice that you're uploading trash, what do you think happens next? That's right. You're going to be banned. You're no longer going to have access to your channel. In fact, your channel may go bye bye, so don't even do it. Instead, focus on value. Look at your niche list, learn everything about your niche and then look for videos that people would want to view.

These are videos that talk about topics people are looking for. How do you do this? Well, first of all, you already have your target keywords. Go to YouTube and look for videos that target those keywords. That's the first thing you do. You're not looking to reinvent the wheel. Instead, you're looking to improve on what already exists.

Pay attention to the videos that others have made. Where did they fail? Did they present incomplete information? Is there stuff outdated? Are their videos too short? Are their images too blurry? Do they use stolen material? Whatever the case may be, identify their strong points and areas for improvement. Build on their areas of improvement and come up with your own videos.

Picking out which videos to make

Now that you have a clear idea of the topics of the videos you're going to be making and your script for those videos, here comes the hard part. What type of video will you be making for YouTube? There are really three major types. You have to select among these carefully.

Face with clips and images

The first type of video is pretty straightforward. It's a video featuring your face, talking to the camera, getting all excited, and in between your presentation, there will be clips and images. For example, if you're talking about a product that you're reviewing, once you start talking about the product, a clip would show up, it shows the product in operation and then you talking over the said clip.

It can also be a static image or a diagram, but your voice will be over the image. The big advantage of using this type of video is you get to connect with your viewer. They can see a face and they can connect it with the brand that you are building. They can see whether they can trust your face or not.

Now, the problem with this is you have to be a good speaker. You can't just look at a script and fumble. That will look unprofessional. You also have to look straight into the camera and look confident and at ease. That's very hard for a lot of people. A lot of people, believe it or not, are not comfortable in their skin.

Also, you have to do this smoothly. You can't just look down on your notes, look at the camera, look at your notes, and stammer. That's not going to work. This takes quite a bit of practice. The good news is, if you keep at it, you will get smoother. The first few videos will probably be rough. But the more videos your produce, the more comfortable you get with the production process, you start connecting the dots, you start innovating, and sooner or later, you look very confident, slick and smooth.

Another downside to this involves self-confidence issues. If you have a few extra pounds or you have bad skin or maybe you have some sort of scar or you got a little bit crazy with the tattoos, this might make you feel that you're not attractive enough to make personal spokesperson type videos.

Well, get those doubts out of your head. You only need to look at the different YouTube channels that currently exist to know that people would watch anything. There are people who are not all that attractive. But as long as they know what they're talking about and people can be confident that they are getting correct information, people wouldn't care what you look like.

Don't think that just because you look far from ideal or your voice isn't all that commanding or smooth, that you have no business making videos. Personally, I've checked out all sorts of video spokespersons on YouTube and they run the gamut. Some are very slick, good-looking, and everything is very well-polished. But, guess what? Their audience isn't as big as some people who are obviously not all that attractive. Don't get stuck on looks. Focus instead on passion.

Whiteboard with animation

Another type of YouTube you can make is a simple whiteboard with animation and voiceover. Basically, you buy software like VideoScribe and you read your script. Once you've created your audio, you then run the software to plug in images to match the audio. VideoScribe would then animate the whole sequence so that a hand is creating all sorts of illustrations you speak.

Whiteboards have been around for a while and they are quite effective. The downside to this is you have to spend a lot of time picking out the right images. Also, VideoScribe in particular, doesn't ship with a large selection of images. Some people are kind of irritated with whiteboard animations because they seem to have the same pictures.

I'm just letting you know that it advance. The obvious workaround here, of course, is to hire an artist to create new pictures and drawings for you, so you can mix things up. Also, if you are not all that confident with you voice, you can hire professional voiceover artists. This is always an option at Fiverr.

The downside to this is a lot of them are actually quite expensive. Sure, you're paying $5, but you only get 50 words. I'm sure your video is going to be more than 50 words. It's not unusual for videos to involve speech of a thousand words or more. Depending on the voiceover artist you hire, this can be a very expensive proposition and I'm just talking about paying for the voice, not a video spokesperson.

Slideshow with voiceover

This is my personal favorite. I like talking into a mic, but I don't like showing my face. I'm also not a big fan of whiteboard animations because, let's face it, if you've seen one, it's very easy to think that you've seen them all. I know that sounds harsh and I definitely sounds biased in my assessment, but to me, this is true.

The great thing about slideshows with voiceovers is that each slideshow is very different. How come? Well, it all boils down to your script and the images that you show with the slideshow. It doesn't get any simpler than that. Now, the problem here is the voiceover. If you are not confident with your voice or you feel like you are stammering all the time, you might have to hire a professional voiceover artist.

Again, as I've mentioned above, this can become very expensive very quickly. This is why I suggest that you start practicing speaking in front of a mic. Sure, at first it may seem rough and it might seem to you to be downright unnatural. But eventually, if you keep reading your script and start getting comfortable with the process, sooner or later, it will just come to you.

When I speak in front of a mic, 99% of the time I just improvise. I only have a few short words on a piece of paper and that's enough for me to talk about everything under the sun. Now, can you imagine specializing in a niche. If you know that niche like the back of your hand, you only need a few words on a sheet of paper in front of you or in a Microsoft Notepad file in front of you and you will be talking up a storm.

That's how slideshows with voiceovers work. It doesn't have to be perfect. It doesn't have to be smooth. You don't have to be the second coming of Ben Affleck to pull this off.

Boost your videos' quality with these little extras

Once you have created a nice-looking video, take it to the next level by adding these little extras. First, invest in a professional intro or outro. An intro and an outro are basically just animations that play right before your presentation or right after. The great thing about an intro and outro is that it draws attention to your brand. It also quickly separates you from your competitors because it lets your viewers know that you are different enough to have invested in an outro and an intro.

I know it may seem like a small thing and in the big scheme of things it may not seem to be that big of a deal, but let me tell you, if you are looking to separate yourself or stand out from the competition, every little bit helps. The next thing you should look into are professional diagrams and graphics.

If you are explaining a fairly complicated topic, you should bite the bullet and go on Fiverr and hire a professional graphics designer to come up with simplified diagram of graphic. You have to understand that a picture is worth a thousand words. Instead of wasting a thousand words explaining some sort of concept, spend a little money on a picture that simplifies everything and drives home the point the first time around.

Finally, you might want to invest in video clips. Even if you are showing slideshows, you can take their quality to the next level if you intersperse or edit in short one-second or half a second-video clips. There are many libraries that offer free video clips or royalty-free video clips. Take advantage of those.

This way, when people watch your video, they see a full product that speaks to them on many different levels. The slicker the overall package, the higher the likelihood you will build a solid brand on YouTube. Since you are scaling up your passive income empire with a firm foundation provided by your YouTube videos, don't be surprised if this all leads to you making a lot more money later on.

Comment on related channels' videos

Now that you have uploaded at least three niche targeted high quality videos to your channel, the next step is to start promoting. How do you do this? Actually, it's quite simple. Just go to other channels that are related to your niche. If you talk about raising backyard chickens, you go to channels dedicated to raising backyard chickens.

If you talk about different breeds of goats and how to prepare goat meat recipes, go to those types of channels. Now, when you're on those related channels, engage with the video maker. Basically tell them, "I like this part of the video, but this could use a little bit more help. Here are my ideas." In other words, contribute something real. Don't just say, "Hey, buddy. You've produced an awesome video. Can you link to me or can you mention me in your next video?" That's not going to fly. You're spamming when you do that.

Instead, to get something, you have to first give something. This is why you have to give value. Since you are, at some level or other a niche expert, that is precisely the kind of value you should be contributing. Let the person producing these niche videos know how they can improve their stuff or what kind of trivia you can contribute that would add value to their channel.

If they see that you keep doing this and they see you as one of the few commenters who are actually credible and authoritative, this may open all sorts of opportunities. Maybe you can cross videoblog. In other words, they would shoot a video of them interviewing you showing off information about your channel and you can do the same for them.

When you do that, you swap audiences. Since they probably have a larger audience because they started off earlier, you have more to gain.

Promote your video on social media and other platforms

In addition to being active on YouTube's comment sections, you should also promote your videos on social media. In the later portions of this guide, I'm going to step you through the process of setting up your social media accounts. This is a good time to set up those accounts if for nothing else to distribute your YouTube on them.

Now, the key here is to distribute the YouTube video link, not the actual video itself. Facebook is notorious for viralizing videos that have essentially been ripped off from YouTube. When you do that, you don't make any money from the views. There is no way you can make money for that because there are no ads surrounding your raw video on Facebook.

Always remember to call your viewers to action

Now that your video looks very professional and talk about the right things, get people to subscribe. Here is the problem. You create an awesome video and you add a lot of value to people's lives, that's great. But the problem is, a lot of people just take the information and then they leave. They don't do anything for you.

Now, last time I checked, people do not produce high quality videos on YouTube or elsewhere because they have nothing else better to do. They're doing it because they want to make money. There's no shame in that. Do yourself a big favor and call your viewers to action. Tell the to subscribe and most importantly, once they've subscribed, to click the bell icon.

When they do that, they get an email update whenever you upload a new video. This brings more eyeballs to your new videos and from these you can promote your older ones.

Boost your videos' earning power

Depending on your niche, YouTube might not pay you money. I know this is a let-down and it definitely sounds depressing. But depending on your niche, YouTube sometimes is more likely demonetize your channel. If this happens, understand that this is not the end of the world. You can set up a Patreon account.

This is a specialized platform where people can agree to send you money via PayPal every single month. In exchange for that subscription, you give them custom videos, you name them on your videos or you give them some sort of freebie. Patreon is a lifesaver because it sets up a system where your community gets to subsidize your content creation.

Now, of course, the secret here is to grow your community. The more Patreon members you get, the more cash you have at the end of the month. Believe me, there's a big difference between 10 Patreon patrons paying $5 each, every month, and 10,000 Patreon patrons paying the same amount of money. Obviously, you know which situation you would rather be in.

It's also a good idea to mention your Patreon patrons at the beginning and at the end of every video. When you do this, you subliminally program your viewers about the benefits of being a patron. Maybe they get T-shirts. Maybe they get some sort of premium item. Maybe they get mentions. Maybe they get a digital badge.

Whatever the case may be, may it look like they're getting a real value for being a patron and they're not just doing it for purely symbolic purposes. When you do this, you increase the perceived value of your channel. It becomes personal to people.

Chapter 6: How to Effectively Set Up Your Brand's Online Platform

In this chapter, I'm going to talk about the passive income model many passive income guides start with. What makes my book different is that I started with videos. Most passive income systems or books that claim to help you build systems start with your blog. I do it the other way around.

The reason why is because when you shoot a video, a lot of the times, you're just saying stuff off the top of your head. Sure, you have a script, but the script is really just a set of talking points. You're just verbalizing the stuff you already know. This is stuff that you're passionate about.

I start with videos because you're not going to be re-shooting over and over again. You're probably going to shoot the video in one take.

This is a big deal because when you write, it's not uncommon for you to go over the same topic again and again. You end up editing yourself. What should have taken only an hour to do takes the whole day.

Believe me, I have found this out in the worst way possible. After all, I started out as a freelance writer. It's too easy to burn a tremendous amount of time manually writing blog post after blog post. You probably have better things to do.

The alternative to this is to put a camera in front of your face and just talk about a topic right off the top of your head in one take. This forces you to be focused, concentrated and effective.

Does it work immediately the first time around? Of course, not. Nothing awesome happens overnight. But the more you create videos, the smoother it all becomes.

I insist that you do that first so that by the time you create a blog and you're going to be writing out a lot of your stuff, you've already become a more disciplined thinker. Do you see how that works? Do you see the genius in this sequence? Good.

Create a Blog Home for Your Brand

Why should you build a blog in the first place? Well, if you're cranking out one video after another, you're building a brand. But the problem is, your channel can only go so far. Eventually, people would look for written words. People would look for a list of resources that are printed. Also, you want to use that collection of printed work as the home of your brand.

Put simply, regardless of where your audience can find you on the internet, they can always refer back to your blog. That's how awesome and powerful your blog can be. It is the home of your brand.

What do you put in your brand's home? Well, you can post your finished videos. You can also post discussions regarding ideas for blog posts. This way, you can interact with your community members and audiences.

You can also direct traffic from your videos to your blog, and vice versa. You can generate content on your blog and then promote it using social media, and vice versa.

For example, you can post questions on Twitter and people would send their responses. Maybe they would respond all at once, or they would respond in drips and drabs. Whatever the case may be, you get all this content. And then you piece it together and then post it on your blog, and then retweet it on social media.

There are just so many ways you can go about doing this, and it all goes back to what I talked about in building systems. You want to create an interlocking flow of traffic and content so that you end up recycling traffic. You end up creating a chain reaction of content creation opportunities.

And the best part to all of this is that the more of this goes on, the more solid your brand becomes.

Build a Mailing List to Hang On to Your Traffic

My most favorite part of having a blog is the fact that it is a natural home for your mailing list. Why? Well, when people read your content, they will be in a position to know whether you know what you're talking about or not. They will be in a position to know whether you are credible and authoritative.

This is important because with your videos, they might only watch just one video, or they might bounce after a few seconds of your video clip. They would not be in a position to know whether you know your stuff or not.

Like it or not, your blog gives you a relatively long amount of time to convince your reader of your expertise. This gives enough of an opportunity to invite them to sign up for your mailing list. Once they've done so, you get to recycle your traffic.

Please understand that the vast majority of people who visit your blog will never come back. They operate on a purely one and done system. They go there once, they check out what they want to check out, and they're gone for good. When you get some of those people to sign up for your mailing list and you send out an update featuring a link to your newest blog post, you get to recycle some of that traffic.

Now, not all of them would show up, but if enough of them shows up, this can give you a nice traffic search. This would get you a lot more traffic over the long haul than you would normally organically pull from the rest of the internet.

Also, when your mailing list reaches a certain size, you can start sending out updates that upsell your members. These updates can contain affiliate links to products that pay you a commission, or they can contain links to your own products and you keep all of your earnings. The earnings possibilities are limitless.

Finally, when you have a mailing list, you can sell solo ads. These are ads placed by other people in your niche who want to target your list members.

For example, if you have a mailing list of people who want to build their muscles organically, then don't be surprised if you get solo ad offers from natural and organic muscle-building supplement makers.

These people would pay for a special ad blast to your mailing list. That ad blast would only have their information, and nothing else. That's why it's called a solo ad.

These can be quite lucrative if a high enough percentage of your list members actually convert. These solo ad advertisers can pay top dollar.

Other Ways to Earn with Your Blog

As I've mentioned, your blog should be the online home of your brand. It shouldn't just be a repository of your content, but should be ground zero of all your branding and content engagement activities. If you view your blog this way, then earning with your blog gets easier.

How exactly can you earn with your blog? Well, you can put ads on your blog. Now, this seems pretty straightforward, but there's actually a lot to this. There are many different types of ads you can put. Here's a short description of each.

Contextual

Contextual ads actually "read" the keywords in a specific page of content on your blog. It will then show ads that have some of those keywords. The thinking is, if there is a good connection between the ad and the content on your blog, then people would click through and possibly buy something.

Contextual ads like Adsense pay you per click. Now, depending on the commercial value of the keywords in your niche, your Adsense earnings can be quite substantial. It can range from a couple of hundred dollars per month to a couple of thousand dollars per month.

CPA

CPA or cost per acquisition ads are a special type of affiliate ads. These ads look like email collection forms or regular graphic ads.

When a reader sees a banner promising a free McDonald's burger or free airline tickets for filling out a form, they click on the ad, and then they are presented with a form. Maybe the form is for insurance, maybe it's for something else. Regardless, if they fill out the form completely enough, you get paid a fairly decent bounty.

Now, depending on the particular offer and depending on the country of the person filling out the form, this can easily add up to dozens of dollars. Can you imagine getting hundreds of sign-ups per day at a few dozen dollars per pop? It doesn't take a rocket scientist to see how lucrative this can be. Of course, it all depends on the quality of your traffic and your niche.

Ads for Your Own Kindle Books

One of the passive income systems that I will be teaching in this book involves publishing Kindle books. In a way, Kindle books are just like blogging. You write once, but you can earn many times with what you've written.

How come? Well, that content can attract traffic. And when that traffic clicks on ads, you may make money.

Now, with Kindle, you write a book and place it on Amazon. If people on Amazon find your book and buy it, you make money.

The same principle applies. You work once, but you can make money many times over from the asset you created by working only once.

Ads for Your Udemy Courses

You can also place ads for courses you put up on Udemy. These are videos that you shoot and you upload on Udemy. When people sign up for your course, Udemy gives you a percentage. You can then promote these courses on your blog.

Dropshipping Ads

You can also advertise physical products that you sell from your dropship store. I'm going to teach you how to set up your own dropshipping business later on in this book. Regardless, you can use your blog as a traffic source for your dropship business, thanks to your ads.

How to Promote Your Blog

Promoting your blog is the most important part of blogging. A lot of older blogger guides out there try to trick you into thinking that you only need to write the very best content and everybody else will beat a path to your door. Boy, I wish it were that easy. Life would be so much simpler if that was the case.

But that's not the case. You can create the very best content. I'm talking about the greatest content since sliced bread. But if people don't know that that content exists or your content has very limited visibility to the rest of the internet, people are not going to care. It's that simple.

So do yourself a big favor, invest 80% of your blogging time to promotions, and 20% to blog content creation. You read that right. This is not a typo.

A lot of guides out there have it completely opposite. They say that you should focus more on content creation and don't worry about promotion. Absolutely wrong. You have to create the very best content, but you have to also spend most of your time promoting it. That's how it works.

So how exactly do you promote your blog content? First, create social media accounts. I suggest that you don't spread yourself too thin. I suggest that you focus on the big platforms like Facebook pages, Facebook groups, Twitter, possibly Pinterest, of course you're already on YouTube, and maybe you should do Instagram as well.

But outside of these major platforms, you should be very stingy with your time. After all, if you don't have money, you're investing time.

So create those social media accounts. Make sure they look professional. Whatever YouTube cover you have must look like your blog header and your blog graphical brand. And then replicate this using the covers of your other social media accounts.

Once you got that out of the way, invest some time in writing the very best bios for those social media accounts. Don't just copy and paste the same garbage over and over again. Let people know on Twitter that you offer a special value on Twitter. Let people know on Facebook that you offer a special value on Facebook.

Once you have customized your descriptions, then comes the easier part. The easier part, of course, is content curation.

Here's the Secret

How do you get traffic off social media? Here's the secret that a lot of people completely miss: you can use other people's content. There, I said it.

This is not stealing, mind you. It's not like you're copying and pasting their content and passing it off as your own work. No. That would be stealing. Instead, you take their link, you come up with a description, and then you publish it on all your social media accounts.

It creates a win-win situation. They win because they get traffic. That much is easy to understand. You win, believe it or not, because you used your expertise and built credibility by picking the very best content related to your niche.

The fact that this content was not made by you doesn't matter. What matters is that the content adds value to the lives of people looking for content in your target niche. This is called curation. You take this third party content and populate all your social media accounts with it.

Now, here's the secret. You don't drop it all at once. You use an auto-publication tool like Hootsuite or Buffer to publish to all your social media accounts on a fixed schedule.

The secret here is to look at the engagement patterns of each account to see what time of day is best for publishing your content. Stick to that time window to maximize your engagement levels.

Still, you curate only the highest quality content, then you promote this content on other related pages, groups and Twitter accounts through engagement. You're going to have to do this manually and you're going to have to do this piecemeal.

But sooner or later, as you target more hashtags and as your curated content makes the rounds, more people would follow your accounts.

Once you have built a decent following, this is when you start rotating in your own blog content. This also includes your videos. And then eventually, you should also post direct calls to action for people to join your mailing list or to click on actual affiliate marketing ads.

Throughout this whole process, you should be researching hashtags that are directly related to your niche. You should target those hashtags in all your social media posts.

Please understand that when you're promoting your blog, your social media accounts should not just be extensions of your blog. They have to have a life of their own. They have to speak to the specific needs of people on a specific platform.

For example, if you are on YouTube, speak to the needs of YouTube users. If you are on Pinterest, offer content that is Pinterest-specific. Don't just copy and paste.

If you do this right, you will get traffic from all these social media platforms heading to your blog, and some of that traffic ending up converting into list members.

Chapter 7: Write Once, Earn Multiple Times

By this point, you probably already know how passive income works: you create an asset once but you stand to earn many times from that asset. This is very easy to see with a YouTube video. You only take one time to record and create the video. Once you upload it on YouTube, over time, people would view the video and there's a good chance that video will earn you some money.

Either it earns you money directly in the form of the earnings that you get from YouTube or the video gets people excited about your affiliate links in the description section of your video. Whatever the case may be you make the video once and you earn many times from it.

The same applies to your blog. You post up content and it continues to attract traffic different parts of the Internet. Over time, people click on ads or do all sorts of things that lead to you making money. That's how it works.

By this point, you can take things to the next level. That's right. I'm talking about books. By writing a book once, you can earn many times over from that single book.

The best place to do this is the Amazon Kindle self-publishing platform. Amazon is huge. It has a tremendous amount of traffic. It has a lot of people who use its Kindle e-book reading device. Given these advantages, Kindle is a logical place to start.

You don't have to stop there. There are many other self-publishing platforms. As long as you learn the ropes on Kindle, you can scale by publishing the same book on other platforms.

Own Niche Verticals on Kindle

If you followed the previous steps in this book properly, your videos should have made you an expert in your niche. At the very least, you know enough about your niche to be some sort of authority or credible expert.

Don't let that expertise go to waste. Write a book in the different segments of your niche. These are segments that people ask questions about and which have a tremendous demand.

Create a Kindle Series of Books

I'm saying that you shouldn't just write one book on your niche. If you look at your niche and slice and dice it and break it down to all its different parts, there are tons of reasons why people would buy specific books addressing specific issues.

You should create a series of these books, and each time you write a book, you reinforce your credibility. The more books you have in a particular niche in Kindle, the greater your niche authority.

Mention your books in your social media profiles. Mention your books in your blog as well as in your videos. Again, the whole point here is to create an online passive income system where each part of the system reinforces other parts.

Your Kindle books should talk about your YouTube channel, your social media accounts and your blogs. So, when people like your book, they can end up on those places. On those platforms, talk about your Kindle books. Promote them so whatever following you develop on those platforms, a certain percentage might end up buying your books.

Promotions Using Kindle

Did you know that by simply publishing books on the Kindle platform, you can pull traffic from that platform to the rest of your online passive income empire? Seriously. I've hinted about this above but here is the nitty-gritty.

Within your Kindle book, you can use it to promote your mailing list. You should call your reader to action and ask them "If you want to be part of an e-mail-based community that talks about these issues or gets the latest and greatest information about this niche or the latest news, sign up for my mailing list."

This takes all of one sentence. It doesn't take much effort, but you have to put it in right part of your book. Don't put it in the front of your book. The front of your book should be all about selling your book. Once people buy your book, get them to read the whole book and then in the end, get people excited about your mailing list.

Similarly, you can use your books to drive traffic to your blog. There are two ways to do this. You can just promote your blog the way you promote your mailing list: with a single sentence.

If you're more creative and you're more insistent, the better way to do this is to drive traffic to your blog within the content of your book. In other words, if people finish a certain section, you call people to action regarding getting more information about the specific subtopic. They just need to click a link and they find themselves on a blog post that talks about that precise subtopic.

Do this for all the subtopics in your book and you create more traffic for your blog, and your blog might get more ad clicks which leads to you making more money.

It goes without saying that you should include your video links in your books. It's really important to put video links in your books to give a much-needed multimedia "push" to your book's content. When people see that your content comes in different forms, they are more likely to find you credible. They are more likely to think that you truly are an expert in your field.

Don't forget to put a link to your Udemy course at the back of your book.

Once people read your whole book, chances are they probably are in a position to honestly determine whether you are a real expert or not. If you did your homework correctly and have persuaded them that you know what you're talking about, they are more likely to sign up for your course.

If they we want to learn more about the topic or they want to learn how to do something that's related to the topic of your book, they can sign up for your Udemy course. This is a logical place to upsell people to your online courses.

The same applies to whatever physical products you're selling through your blog courtesy of your dropship business. If your books talks about certain problems, hype up physical products that they can use to fix those problems.

This is where your dropshipping store comes in. You don't just mention a product. You mention specific solutions and people can take action on those solutions by clicking on a link and they go straight to your dropship site.

Finally, you can also promote your social media accounts in your books. Tell them that if they're looking for the latest and greatest update or cutting-edge information, they only need to follow you on Twitter, Instagram, Facebook groups or Facebook pages among many others.

How to Promote Your Book

In keeping with the interlocking traffic and content system that I described in an earlier part of this book, promoting your Kindle book is actually pretty forward. How? You just plug it in to the rest of the passive income system you have built. If you have a blog, a certain percentage of the ads you're automatically showing on your blog must be your book.

Now, here's the secret. Do not show banner ads. That's right. Don't show graphics. Your ads should be text ads. People are more likely to click on these.

Also, you have a lot more leeway because you can get creative in the titles and colors of these ads. You also can give yourself quite a bit of real-estate space in terms of the description for your book.

Similarly, in your video, you should have certain fixed spots where you show the actual cover of your book, and you should talk about your book. At the bottom of that cover should be a shortened URL. You can easily get these from bit.ly.

The shorter your URL, the better. So, when people type in the URL from your video or they click on the shortened URL in the description portion of your video, they end up on your Amazon Kindle sales page.

You can also promote one Kindle book on other Kindle books. In other words, when you publish older books, each newer book should promote the older looks. It can be as simple as listing your name and saying you're the author of Books 1, 2, 3, 4 and 5, and each of these books should have a short, mini description in your newest book. When another book comes out after that book, guess what? It's going to have that book's description in addition to your previous books.

This way, every time you publish on Kindle, you get many bites at the apple. You get another opportunity not only to promote the specific book you just published but all the other books that you have published previously.

Next, you should promote your Kindle book on your mailing list. Either you send out a live update, which is basically a spur-of-the-moment kind of thing, or you can set up an automated publishing system where after a few days have passed since a new list member joined your list, they would get a certain e-mail, then after a few days they would get another e-mail. Regardless of how you do it, your mailing list is a great way to get people to know about your book and possibly buy it.

Finally, you can promote your Kindle book through auto-publishing on your social media accounts. As I mentioned earlier, you can use tools like Hootsuite to schedule your curated content posts on your social media accounts. This is a big deal. You don't have to be there to manually publish at a certain time.

Now, use this to its fullest potential by publishing posts that link directly to your link shortener. This way, people can click directly to end up on your Kindle sales page.

Chapter 8: Monetize Your Expertise-the Right Way!

As I mentioned earlier, one way to make passive income is to sell online courses. I'm not just talking about written materials here. I'm talking about posting videos of you teaching the viewer how to do things. Believe it or not online courses sell really well.

The best platform for this is also the most popular. I am talking about Udemy.com. There are tons of courses there, but don't let this fact scare you. The fact that it has so many courses is a testament to its drawing power. It has hundreds of thousands of students.

How do you make passive income with Udemy? It's actually quite simple. You create your video course once. So, you shoot it once in a series, and once all the materials are done, and this includes both video and course materials like your syllabus and your handouts and your tests, you upload it to Udemy and you're done.

People can see your course. They can see your sales video. They can see a snippet of what you have to offer as well as your syllabus. If they like what they see, they sign up.

You don't have to physically show up to teach the course. You just record yourself once. So, it's possible that you recorded yourself several years back and you're still making hundreds, if not thousands, of dollars off that same course month after month, year after year. How awesome is that?

Here's how you do it.

Break Down Your Niche and Sell Courses in Each Section

The first thing that you need to do is to look at your niche and understand that there are certain parts of your niche that are very hot. These are the parts that a lot of people want instruction in. Now, the downside to this is that these are the parts that also already have a lot of competition on Udemy.

You should then look at sub-niches that don't have as much competition. Focus on these sub-niches. Create specialized courses on them.

Your competitors might be fighting over the most in-demand niches. You, on the other hand, scoop up the lion's share of demand for sub-niche topics. This way, you're not attacking your competitors where they're strongest.

They've been on Udemy far longer than you. They probably have a more recognizable brand. These are very hard advantages to overcome.

So, hit them where they're weak. Hit them at the sub-niche. Sell courses in each of those sub-niches.

The best part to all of this is many niches have so many sub-niches that you can actually create different mini-courses for each of these sub-niches. With each course, you can then talk about the fact that you are teaching other sub-niche courses so these videos tend to reinforce each other. Not only can you drive people to sign up to course after course, but you also end up repeatedly branding yourself as a credible authority because you have so many courses on Udemy.

How to Make Money with Your Courses

Not only would your many video courses on Udemy reinforce each other's value and thereby drive up your course earnings; you can also use each course as a selling platform. How do you pull this off?

Well, you can upsell your blog. From time to time, you can say in a video that you have a blog so if people have any questions or if people want further discussion regarding a topic that you just explained, they can go straight to your blog or you can even mention a specific URL in your blog where they can get more information.

Similarly, you can upsell your Kindle books. You can tell them "This is all you need to know about this topic, but if you really want to drill deep or if you want to look at the broader implications or if you want to be a master at this type of thing, here's my Kindle book." You can drop the Kindle link in both video as well as in the body of the course.

Finally, you can also upsell your dropship items. If you're selling physical products, you can mention different alternative ways of doing things in your course. Of course, the goal here is to get the viewer to think that doing things manually is a hassle. You then present your physical product as some sort of shortcut.

You then mention the features of the product and how it either speeds things up or it increases the quality of their work product or otherwise makes their life more convenient. You than mention the link both in your written materials as well as in the body of your video.

How to Promote Your Udemy Courses

Promoting your Udemy course is actually pretty straightforward once you have an infrastructure built. If you have videos on YouTube, this is the first place you're going to be promoting your Udemy course. Since your YouTube videos are, by definition, episodic and tend to be nitpicky, in other words, they take a sub-niche with all its many issues and then focus only on an issue or two.

So, when you present that type of video, it's packed with a lot of value. However, when people watch your video, you tell them "If you really want to drill down and get to the nitty-gritty, I'm teaching a course on this. Take the course and you'll be an expert like me."

This is a powerful way of using your existing video infrastructure to upsell your Udemy course. When they sign up for you Udemy course, on the other hand, you also upsell them on your other products. Do you see how this works? This is what you get when you build a system instead of just engaging in one hack after another.

Also, you can use your social media accounts to promote your Udemy course. Using curated content, you can blast out all these materials. People then click through to find your Udemy course listings. The more credible you become on different social media platforms, the easier it would be for them to find your Udemy courses.

Your blog is also a great place to promote your Udemy course. It's actually pretty easy to do this. I suggest that you use text links instead of graphic banners. The text links should be put in the right places in your blog posts.

For example, if you have posted something about how to do something, you then put a link saying "If you want to be an expert in this or if you want to and learn how to do this for money, sign up for my course". Then, when they click, they end up at your Udemy course.

Of course, you have to set this up properly. You can't just drop the link everywhere. You have to set it up so that people who are mostly likely to want to sign up for a course will see your link. You just don't do this casually.

Finally, you can promote your Udemy course in your Kindle books. Again, there has to be a tight niche correlation between the Kindle book and the specific course you are promoting.

For example, if you are teaching people how to make money day-trading stocks, the link in that Kindle book must go to a Udemy course that goes beyond the basics of day-trading. The video training should involve actual signals people have to read so they can make real money with day-training.

In other words, the book starts as some sort of qualifier book. These are people who may be interested in day-trading or maybe not. They're basically dipping their toes in the water and trying to figure out what they feel about the topic.

When you upsell them to your Udemy course, you're upselling a specific type of people. These are people who have actually made a decision to try to make a living with day-trading. Do you see the difference?

Chapter 9: New Default Settings to Scale Up Your Passive Income

Regardless of whether you're doing YouTube, Udemy, bogging or Kindle books, you must do this at all times. I am, of course, talking about making money off advertising. You should do affiliate marketing at all times.

Affiliate Marketing Basics

What is affiliate marketing anyway?

Well, affiliate marketing is a system where a product creator will pay you a certain percentage of the sale they make from the product they sold because you referred traffic to them. Your job is to drive traffic to an affiliate link. If that traffic converts, you get a bounty. It can be a fixed amount of money or it can be a percentage of a sale.

You can also make money when people download a piece of software or when they enter their e-mail address. There's really not much difference. It all boils down to you getting paid for driving traffic.

There are three variations to this.

The first is CPA. CPA can take the form of making money per sales acquisition. You show ads on your blog or text links in your YouTube channel or your Kindle book. When people click on the link and they buy something, you get paid. If they click on a link and they see an e-mail collection page and they enter their e-mail, you make money.

Similarly, some programs pay you per click. When people see native ads which look like pictures or article ads on your blog and they click it, you can make as much as twenty-five to even fifty cents per click.

Finally, there's also e-mail-based income. I created a separate section for this because sometimes people will pay you for the honor of showing their ads to your mailing list members. This is a big deal because advertisers are looking for specialized audiences.

If you have built a mailing list, chances are the people who are on your list are interested in only a specific topic. They don't care about anything else. This makes them the ideal audience for advertisers who deal in those topics. These advertisers will pay you per e-mail blast.

For example, if you have a mailing list made up of a hundred thousand people, somebody may pay you a thousand dollars to e-mail those people. The understanding is a high-enough percentage of those people will open their e-mails and of those, a high-enough percentage will click on links. Of the link clickers, a high-enough percentage will actually buy from the e-mail by clicking on a link to load up a sales page.

If everything goes right, the advertiser would make a lot more than the thousand dollars they paid you to advertise their ad. If that's the case, don't be surprised if they keep coming back to you to buy solo ad after solo ad. That's how e-mail-based income works.

The key here is the quality of your mailing list. If your mailing is made up of people who actually buy stuff and who are eager buyers, don't be surprised if you not only get more advertisers, but the ad revenue that you make for each solo ad keeps going up.

How to Optimize Your Ads

I wish I could tell you that all affiliate marketing ads above are pretty much equal. I wish I could tell you that CPA, CPC and all their variations are pretty much the same. Unfortunately, if I were to do that, I would be lying to you.

Different ads vary tremendously in terms of revenue generation. Also, different advertisers generate money for you at different levels. Some don't even make you any money.

So, how do you maximize your income from affiliate marketing? It's actually pretty straightforward. Try out all sorts of ads. Let it run for a month then look at your statistics. Pick the top three winners. These are the ones that get the most clicks and the most conversions. Chances are when you do this experiment, you probably will only be able to find the ads that get the most clicks with a few sales. That is good enough.

Once you have identified those, change up their ads or their text links. Mix things up and if you're able to maximize your click-through rate, pick the winning ad variations and then try to maximize your conversions. If you go through this process enough times, you would have optimized your ads so that you are able to make more money from your advertise. You get a lot more clicks which translates to a lot more conversions.

Please don't expect this to happen overnight. You're going to have to pay attention to details. You also have to go through this process several times as you optimize different elements of your ads. This is not exactly something that drops out of the sky or something that you luck into. It takes quite a bit of sustained effort and focus.

Chapter 10: Want to Sell Branded Physical Products? Here You Go!

Make no mistake selling electronic books online is a great thing. Getting people to click on your ads is a good way to make money, but you should not leave any money on the table. You have to understand that people are also looking for physical products. This is stuff that gets shipped to them in a box.

Don't let this moneymaking opportunity slip through your fingers. If you have followed all the chapters above, and you've built a solid brand in your niche, at some point in time, people would love to buy physical products from you bearing your brand. Would you like to get to that stage? Would you like to turn that interest into cold, hard cash?

If your answer is yes, I have the solution for you. The solution is not to buy a tremendous amount of products, put them in specialty packages, slap your brand on them and lease expensive warehouses throughout the United States to store that stuff.

I'm telling if that is your plan of action, you either have to have a lot of money now or you're probably going to go bankrupt sooner rather than later. The old way of doing e-commerce is a non-starter. Handling your own stuff, shipping your own materials, hassling with customers directly - it's a fool's error.

Thankfully, there is a way around this, and it's cheap, quick and effective. I am, of course, talking about dropshipping. Dropshipping is a fulfillment model. Instead of your customer buying something from your store and you picking out the product, putting the product in a package and shipping it to your customer from your warehouse, dropshipping makes things so much smoother.

How? When you get an order, you set up your software to order that item automatically from your source's store. Your source would then directly ship the product to your customer. You don't handle the product at any point.

It is smooth. It is quick. It is seamless. The best part is you don't have to buy product ahead of time. You only turn around and buy the product from your source when your customer shows up and actually pays for the product on your online store. The best part to this is you can mark up the product that you end up selling by a factor of 2:1, 3:1 and even as high as 20:1. I know that sounds crazy and outrageous but it's true.

If you don't believe me, go to AliExpress.com. Take a look around. Compare some of the prices of those products with many online stores, and better yet, offline stores. The margins are just crazy. We're talking about 2:1, 3:1, 4:1 or even 10:1.

That's how solid dropshipping is if you know how to pull it off. In this quick guide, I'm going to take all the mystery out of dropshipping.

Use the Perfect Trifecta

Trifecta? What's that? Well, trifecta is doing three things back to back to produce an awesome result.

By setting up your online store using Shopify, you can quickly put up an online store. You don't have to get your own domain name. You don't have to get hosting. You don't have to hassle with the typical housekeeping chores the typical online store owner has to put up with.

Second, Shopify has a plugin system. These are specialized software that you can order off Shopify that will give special functionality to your online store. You can change the look of your store and, most importantly, you can change its functionalities.

Now, the plugin that I want you to get is Oberlo. With this plugin, you can go to AliExpress with your browser and pick out products you want to sell on my your online store. With a few mouse clicks and keystrokes, you can smoothly and seamlessly import products from AliExpress to your online store, change the descriptions and keep track of inventory. This way, you don't end up in the ridiculous position of selling products your source has run out of.

You then create a brand for your store and pump traffic to your store. If you created a seamless online passive income system, you end up selling a tremendous amount of physical products at a fat profit margin.

By this point, you should have built quite a promotional network for your physical products. You probably would be able to promote your dropship business through your videos, your Kindle books, your blog posts, your mailing list and your Udemy course among many others.

And I'm just talking about one vertical. Maybe you're very industry and diligent and motivated, and you have created different verticals. You can sell your products and all those different articles as well.

Take Things to the Next Level

Believe it or not if you do not have a branded merchandise store on Shopify, you can still make a lot of money. You're essentially just selling a generic product. However, if you want to take your profits to a much higher level, you have to brand your store. This means that everything in your shop is branded.

Now, this will cost you some money because this time, you're going to buy the product and put them in packaging that has your brand. You might even have to put a brand specifically on the product items themselves.

You then ship all these branded materials to Amazon and have Amazon handle the fulfillment. Sure, this is more expensive since it requires cash up front. The good news is you get to enjoy higher profit margins simply because you have a brand on your product.

If you do this right, then your passive online income system will pump all this qualified brand-conscious traffic to your physical product store. How come? Well, each section of your passive online income empire, whether it be your YouTube channel, your Kindle book series, your branded blog, your mailing list or your Udemy course, talk about your brand again and again.

In fact, regardless of where people find you on the Internet, they will come into contact with your brand. Their brand then points to your branded product.

Now, why is this a big deal? Can't they just get a generic product? What's the big deal about brands anyway?

Well, let me tell you if you don't have a brand, you have a commodity. Let's say your online store sells earrings. Do you realize how easy it is to find earrings online? Even if you have a specific type of earring like unicorn earrings, you can easily find those at AliExpress for pennies. That's how cheap they are.

Now, if you have a branded unicorn earring with your specific packaging, people are willing to give you the benefit of the doubt. People are not buying just a generic unicorn earring. Instead, they're buying that earring because it came from you. It has your brand.

Once you have developed yourself into a brand, you can charge a lot more money. If you need proof of this, I want you to wrap your mind around that fact. This is a fact. This is not a theory. This is not a guess. This not speculation. This is a fact.

It costs Nike athletic footwear corporation no more than $5 per pair of sneakers straight from Vietnam. That's all they pay, but guess how much people pay for a pair of Air Jordans in the United States. We're talking over $200. That's the power of branding.

If Nike can do it, you can do it too. It all boils down to you developing a solid brand. You really only have two choices. Either you have a brand or you have a commodity, and I'm telling when you play the commodity game, there's only one way to go and its down because the only feature you can compete on is the price.

Focus on branding and cap off your online passive income empire with your own branded dropship store.

Conclusion

As exciting as the information presented in this book may be, I have some bad news for you. At this point, a lot of people are excited. At this point in the book a lot of people are pumped up. At this point in the book, a lot of people are highly motivated.

Sadly, I've seen this all before, and I'm sorry to report that is not good enough. You may be dreaming of building a massive online passive income where you work only a few hours every single week, and you're making all these dollars. That's awesome!

However, at this point, you have to stop dreaming and start doing. Just do it. I hate to sound like a Nike commercial, but you need to just do it. Potential can only take you so far. Dreaming at a certain point is dead.

You have to do it, and I'm not just talking about doing it in theory or potentially doing it at some point in the future. I'm talking about doing it now. Right here, right now.

In fact, a lot of online passive income coaches say that you should not get ready, aim and fire. I agree with them. You know how I do it? You should just fire, aim and then ready, and then repeat it again and again and again until you keep hitting the mark.

The key is you have brought yourself to the point where you can take action. It's just too easy to get caught up in analysis paralysis. It's just too easy to get caught up in weighing the pros and cons of all these different passive incomes systems until you get lost in the details.

Soon enough, you run out of time because you have all sorts of duties, responsibilities and obligations to attend to. So, what started out as a tremendous amount of motivation and excitement ends up yet another dead project.

It's another one of those things that you could have done or should have done or would have done, but "life got in the way". Stop giving yourself excuses. Fire, aim, ready.

Once you start, please understand that you're not going to hit a home run, okay? You're not going to make a million dollars overnight.

Don't get me wrong. Sometimes that happens. From time to time, people do get lucky. However, for the most part, expect to hit a snag. Expect that it doesn't turn out the way you expected, and that's okay.

Optimize. Learn from your mistakes. Keep taking baby steps forward. Stop, figure out what went wrong and keep going. Sooner or later, you will start making money. It may not be a lot of money, but it will be some money.

Once that happens, reinvest a fixed percentage of your profits. It may be 10%. It may be 20%. Heck! It might even be 50%. Whatever the case may be, be consistent. Every time somebody some way somehow sends you money, a certain percentage must go back to your business. This is how you find the resources to scale up.

There are two ways to scale. You scale up vertically. In other words, you follow my advice in this book. Start with videos then proceed to blog posts then to Kindle books then to Udemy then to your own online store.

Once you have dominated the different sub-niches in your niche and you have become a solid brand, use that same system to scale up vertically. Find other related niches and scale up horizontally then.

Keep repeating this process and sooner or later you would have hundreds of businesses each producing anywhere from a few dozen dollars per month to a few thousand dollars per month. It doesn't take a rocket scientist to figure out that if you aggregate all the incomes of these businesses that have scaled up vertically and horizontally at some level or other, you are looking at some real money.

Finally, think long term. Once you start making solid money with your online passive income system, don't just blow it all on vacations or by taking it easy. Instead, pour some of that cash into domain names, bonds and real estate commercial property passive income. This way, you protect yourself by diversifying your different personal income streams.

I wish you nothing but the greatest success!

Copyright © 2020 by Pollux Andrews

All rights reserved. No part of this book may be reproduced in any form without permission in writing from the author.

No part of this publication may be reproduced or transmitted in any form or by any means, mechanical or electronic, including photocopying or recording, or by any information storage and retrieval system, or transmitted by email or by any other means whatsoever without permission in writing from the author.

DISCLAIMER

While all attempts have been made to verify the information provided in this publication, the author does not assume any responsibility for errors, omissions, or contrary interpretations of the subject matter herein.

The views expressed are those of the author alone and should not be taken as expert instruction or commands. The reader is responsible for his or her own actions.

The author makes no representations or warranties with respect to the accuracy or completeness of the contents of this work and specifically disclaims all warranties, including without limitation warranties of fitness for a particular purpose. No warranty may be created or extended by sales or promotional materials. The advice and recipes contained herein may not be suitable for everyone. This work is sold with the understanding that the author is not engaged in rendering medical, legal or other professional advice or services. If professional assistance is required, the services of a competent professional person should be sought. The author shall not be liable for damages arising here from. The fact that an individual, organization of website is referred to in this work as a citation and/or potential source of further information does not mean that the author endorses the information the individual, organization to website may provide or recommendations they/it may make. Further, readers should be aware that Internet websites listed in this work might have changed or disappeared between when this work was written and when it is read.

Adherence to all applicable laws and regulations, including international, federal, state, and local governing professional licensing, business practices, advertising, and all other aspects of doing business in any jurisdiction in the world is the sole responsibility of the purchaser or reader.

www.ingramcontent.com/pod-product-compliance
Lightning Source LLC
Chambersburg PA
CBHW072025230526
45466CB00019B/550